WHAT WOULD BABU DO?

C. P. Rock

To order additional copies of this book, contact:
Xlibris
844-714-8691
www.Xlibris.com
Orders@Xlibris.com

ISBN: Softcover   979-8-3694-1813-0
         Hardcover   979-8-3694-1815-4
         EBook   979-8-3694-1814-7

Library of Congress Control Number: 2024905320

Print information available on the last page

Rev. date: 03/21/2024

What Would Babu Do?

Safia loved her grandfather and the way he'd swoop her up and set her down on the ground.

"Wheeeee!" She giggled as he swung her up and around before gently setting her down.

She called him Babu. "That's the Swahili word for 'grandfather,'" she was proud to say.

Babu would always tell her, "I'm gonna take you to Africa one day, because where there's a will, there's a way!" Babu called her Biscuit because he said her cheeks were like biscuits with butter.

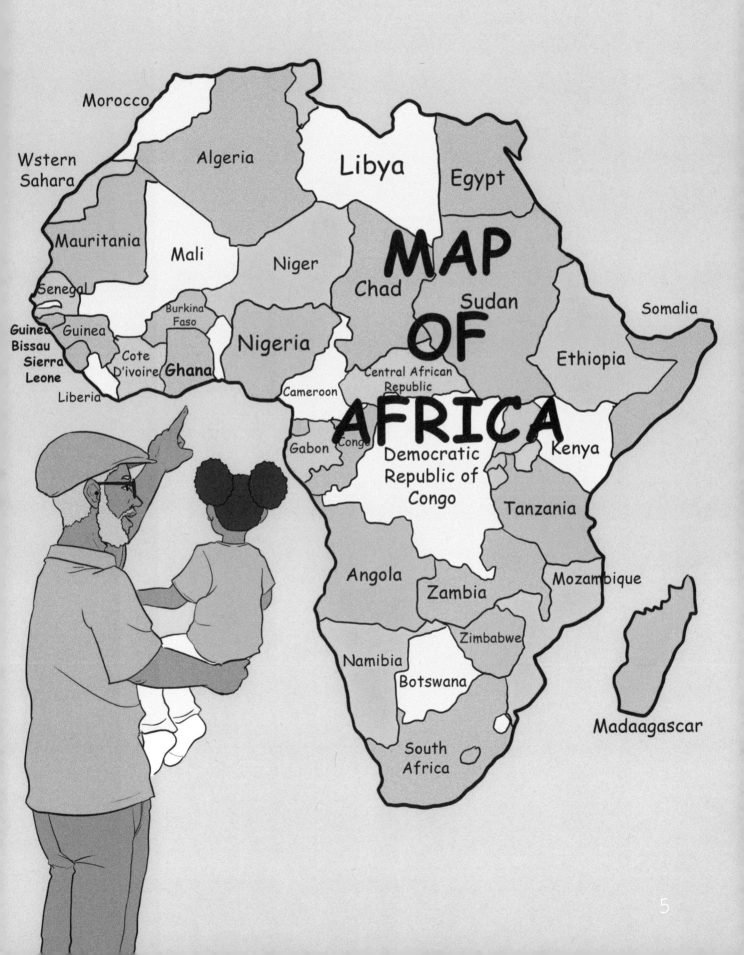

Babu liked to talk in rhymes, and so did Safia. When she was happy and when she was sad, she knew a rhyme would work every time. "I'm going to rhyme like my Babu and just like my Daddy too!"

One afternoon Babu and Safia were at the playground. She was big enough to climb the slide all by herself and take a ride all the way down to the ground. "Whee!" Safia giggled. "Babu, I'm so high up! Do you know what I see? I can see the top of the tree!"

Later, Safia saw something on the playground that made her sad. A little girl was crying because another child said something to the little girl that was bad.

Safia said to herself, "What would Babu do?" Babu always had something to say that was true.

Safia thought about it and then asked the little girl, "Are you OK? Come on over here where we can play."

She put her arm around the little girl and walked her over near where Babu was sitting reading his book; the little girl's grandfather was also reading his book. Safia sang that song Babu always sang: "Everything's Gonna Be Alright, Every Little Thing's Gonna Be Alright." When the little girl heard that, her smile became really, really bright!

Safia remembered that Babu was always nice to other people; he'd say, "I was just being good to them like I hope they will be good to me, you see."

The little girl and Safia played and played and played together until it was time to go that day.

On the way home, Babu said, "Safia, my little Biscuit, I'm so proud of you today because you helped that little girl in your own special way."

When it was time for bed, Babu gave Safia kisses on both of her cheeks and said, "Good night and sleep tight, Biscuit!"

Babu turned out the light, and she closed her eyes. Before she knew it, she was sound asleep.

The next morning Safia heard a sound that woke her up: *peep-peep, peep-peep, peep-peep*. She looked out of her window and saw a little baby birdie on the ground under the tree in the backyard.

Uh oh, Safia thought. *The little baby birdie must have fallen out of its nest. I'm going to call her Sankofa, and I want to help her. I'll do my best.*

Hmmm, she thought. *What would Babu do?* Babu always did something that was true.

Safia went into her closet and took her favorite shoes out of their box. She took her pencil and poked holes in the top. *This way Sankofa can breathe*, she thought.

She tiptoed down the hall and knocked on Babu's door. "Babu, Babu, a little bird fell down out of her nest, and she's on the ground. I named her Sankofa. I have a shoebox with a cover," Safia whispered. "Can you help me save her and give her back to her mother?"

Babu put down his book and said, "Well, Biscuit, we can try. Let's go outside and see whether we can get Sankofa back up in her nest in the tree."

Safia held her shoebox in one hand and held Babu's hand with her other. They opened the side door and walked out into the yard and over to Sankofa. *Peep-peep, peep-peep, peep-peep.* Babu told Safia to put the box down and take off the cover. "We're going to pick Sankofa up gently to let her know that we love her."

He put Safia's hands side by side like a cup inside of his hands, and they scooped Sankofa up together.

They moved slowly and carefully so that they would not ruffle even one little feather.

Babu said, "Biscuit, we're going to wrap Sankofa in a little blanket to warm her so that she'll feel safe and know we won't harm her. Then I'm going to the garage to get my ladder, and we'll do our best to get her back in her nest."

When Babu went to the garage, Safia sang "Everything's Gonna Be Alright, Every Little Thing's Gonna Be Alright" to Sankofa to make her feel better.

Babu set up his ladder, and Safia gave him the box with Sankofa inside. He climbed up the ladder just like Safia climbed her slide. When Babu reached the nest, he said, "Biscuit, I'm so high up! Do you know what I see? I can see the nest in the top of the tree!"

Safia saw Momma Bird on the branch nearby. Momma Bird was a little nervous, but she didn't fly away. She was waiting for Babu to do his best.

"Babu, Babu!" Safia called out. "Momma Bird is waiting for you to put Sankofa in the nest."

Babu came down the ladder and kissed Safia on her cheeks. "Well, Biscuit, Sankofa is safe, and Momma Bird is happy." Babu always said something that was true.

Then he said, "Safia, my little Biscuit, I'm so proud of you today because you helped that little birdie in your own special way."

"Whee!" She giggled as he swung her up
and around before gently setting her down.

She remembered that Babu was always nice to other animals; he said, "I was just being good to them like I hope they will be good to me, you see."

Safia thought, *That's what Babu would do. And I will too!*

Milton Keynes UK
Ingram Content Group UK Ltd.
UKHW050633010424
440413UK00005B/80